NOW YOU CAN READ ABOUT
STRANGE CREATURES

TEXT BY RITA GRAINGE

Y BOB BAMPTON

BRIMAX BOOKS • NEWMARKET • ENGLAND

There are many types of creatures in the world. Some look very strange. Some do strange things.

This strange creature is a sea slug. It floats on the surface and feeds on jellyfish.

The giant anteater has a very long snout. It licks up ants with its sticky tongue.

This animal is
easy to see. It is
a fire salamander.

But you must look
closely to find
this leaf fish.
It stands on its
head and hides in
the weed.

The electric eel does not need to
hide. It can give its enemies
an electric shock.

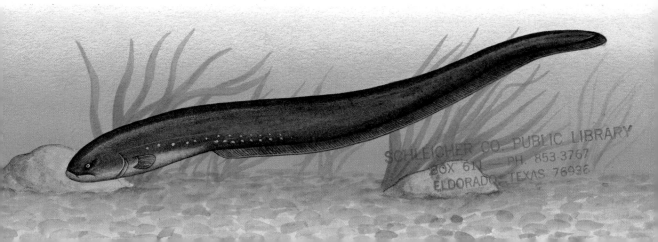

These creatures look odd.

The armadillo has a coat of bony plates. He looks like a knight in armour ready for battle.

This male midwife toad has a batch of eggs stuck to his back legs. He carries them until they hatch into tadpoles.

Spider crabs dress
up in sponge and
weed. This helps
them to hide.

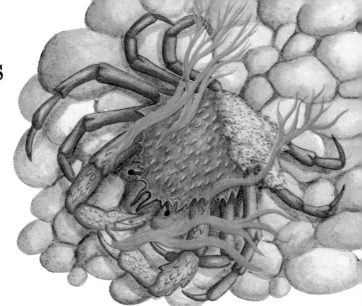

Is this a bird or an animal?
The duck-billed platypus has the
body of an animal but the beak
and webbed feet of a duck.

Look at this strange creature.
The thorny devil lives in
Australia. Its scales are
long and spiky. At night,
dew forms on them.

When young Nile crocodiles hatch
their mother picks them up with
her jaws. She has a special pouch
in the bottom of her mouth. Can
you see the baby crocodile?

Tadpoles look like fish. They grow legs and lose their tails as they change into frogs or toads.

One type of frog grows smaller instead of bigger. The tadpole is longer than your foot. When it becomes a frog it shrinks to the size of your big toe. Nobody knows how or why.

There are many strange creatures in the sea. The dragonfish has long fins spiked with poison. Can you see the puffer fish? It swallows water or air to blow itself up into a thorny ball. No other sea creature will try to eat it. There is an octopus on the seabed.

Look for the brown
fish with a light
on its head. This
is a deep-sea
angler fish.
It droops the
light over its
mouth. Other fish
come close to look
at the light. Then
the angler fish
snaps shut its
sharp teeth.
What other strange
sea creatures can
you find?

Look at these clever creatures.
The chameleon hides from other
animals by changing its colour.
Can you find it?

There are some
animals who play
"dead" when there
is danger. This
opossum is lying
down. It stays
still until its
enemy goes.

The frilled lizard gapes and hisses to scare its attackers. It is harmless really.

Roadrunners are American birds that like running. They run very fast. Look for the snake in the roadrunner's beak. It kills its prey by making a sudden pounce.

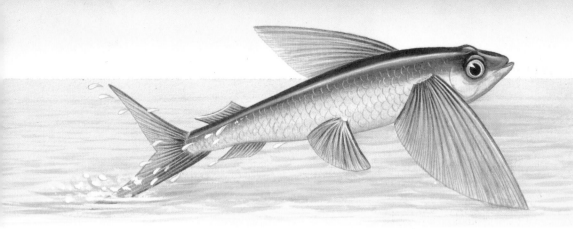

Here is a fish that can fly.
It flaps its fins and flips its
tail. It glides above the sea.

Adult salmon go
back to the river
where they hatched.
They leap up high
waterfalls. At the
head of the river
they lay their eggs
and then die.

The sugar glider
lives in Australia.
It has extra skin
between its front
and back legs.
This helps it to
glide from tree
to tree.

Flying frogs have
webs between their
toes. They glide
from one tree to
another. There are
sticky pads on
their toes. These
help the frog to
hold on when it
lands.

These creatures live in odd places.

Look at the elf
owl in the cactus.
A woodpecker makes
a hole in the
cactus. Then the
elf owl moves in
to make a home.

The female cuckoo
lays her eggs in
other birds' nests.
The cuckoo egg
is bigger. When
the owners return,
they sit on all
the eggs until
they hatch.

Bats hang by their feet with their wings wrapped round their bodies. In winter they hang together in dark places.

The remora has a suction pad on its head. This sticks firmly to a big shark. Remoras have a free ride and feed on food left over.

Can you see the beaver nibbling at the tree trunk? When the tree falls down the beaver nibbles it into small pieces. Then it builds a dam to protect its home.

The beaver's home is called a lodge. It has a hole in the roof to let in air.

A water spider
needs air. It blows
a big air bubble
like a diving
bell. Then it
lives under water
in the bubble.

This is a mouthbrooder fish. The
female carries her eggs inside
her mouth. Look at the young.
When danger is near they return
to their mother's mouth.

Some creatures
have strange
eating habits.
Agoutis often
peel their fruit
before eating it.

This raccoon is
washing its food.

Vampire bats feed
on blood from other
animals. They make
a hole in the
animal's skin with
their four sharp
teeth. Then they
suck out blood.

Snakes open their jaws very wide. Some swallow eggs. Others can swallow a whole animal. Their teeth point backwards. This helps them to pull in the food.

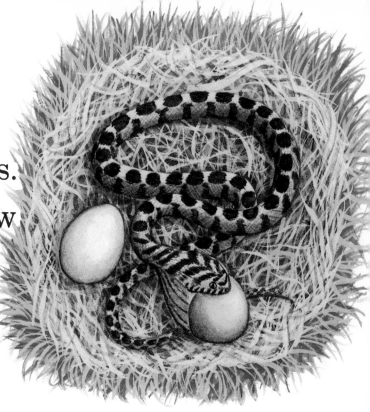

Crocodiles swallow stones to help them stay under the water. This crocodile has its mouth wide open to keep cool. The birds are picking meat from the crocodile's teeth.

Do you know these creatures?
Why are they strange?